DIY PROJECTS
FOR
CATS & DOGS

DIY PROJECTS
FOR
CATS & DOGS

20 Easy-to-Build Creations
for Your Best Friend

Armelle Rau & Pierre Legrix

COMPANIONHOUSE
BOOKS

DIY Projects for Cats & Dogs

CompanionHouse Books™ is an imprint of Fox Chapel Publishers International Ltd.

Project Team
Vice President–Content: Christopher Reggio
Translator: Donna Vekteris
Editor: Colleen Dorsey
Design: Mary Ann Kahn
Index: Jay Kreider

DIY Projects for Cats & Dogs is an unabridged translation of a 2017 French book.
Original title: *Bricolages pour Animaux* © 2017 by Éditions Massin, collection Savoir & Faire – Société d'Information et Créations (SIC)

Project Team (French Edition)
Editorial Director: Thierry Lamarre
Editor: Flore Beaugendre
Proofreader: Isabelle Misery
Project Design/Construction and Step-by-Step Directions: Armelle Rau and Pierre Legrix
Photography: Pierre Nicou
Step-by-Step Photography: Armelle Rau and Pierre Legrix
Stylist: Kathrin Lezinsky
Design and Layout: Either Studio, Sylvain Kaslin

ISBN 978-1-62187-129-3

The Cataloging-in-Publication Data is on file with the Library of Congress.

This book has been published with the intent to provide accurate and authoritative information in regard to the subject matter within. While every precaution has been taken in the preparation of this book, the author and publisher expressly disclaim any responsibility for any errors, omissions, or adverse effects arising from the use or application of the information contained herein.

Fox Chapel Publishing
903 Square Street
Mount Joy, PA 17552

Fox Chapel Publishers International Ltd.
7 Danefield Road, Selsey (Chichester)
West Sussex PO20 9DA, U.K.

www.facebook.com/companionhousebooks

We are always looking for talented authors. To submit an idea,
please send a brief inquiry to acquisitions@foxchapelpublishing.com.

Printed and bound in Singapore
21 20 19 18   2 4 6 8 10 9 7 5 3 1

Introduction

When we are enchanted by some beautiful object we've seen online, on a blog, on Pinterest, or perhaps in a decorating magazine, we may fall in love and decide that we simply must have it. In these moments we have two choices: either buy the original, no matter the cost, even if we end up paying for it over the course of months, or build it ourselves. This is the do-it-yourself principle: when we make things ourselves, we express our creativity and feel joy and pride.

When we—there's always a "we" in the projects in this book—first began making DIY projects for our apartment, we started with a few basic pieces that enhanced our daily lives: a little side table, then a wardrobe that saved us a bundle, then an entire bookcase, and finally lamps. Now, more than half of the furnishings in our apartment in Nantes, France, were made by us.

In this book, you'll find plenty of ideas to simultaneously brighten up your home and please your pet. The furniture we've designed and built is more original and attractive than what you see in pet stores. We've never been able to find store-bought items that keep our cat entertained, hide unsightly necessities, and offer protection, all in one.

In true do-it-yourself spirit, this book combines practicality with a view to keeping costs down. You won't find expensive projects here. We work with found objects, scrap wood, and simple materials. You don't have to be an expert do-it-yourselfer, either. All you need is a little patience and creativity. We provide the basics, and then we leave it up to you to personalize your handiwork.

So put aside Instagram, Pinterest, and the Internet for a little while and rediscover the pleasure of paper and the scent of a brand-new book in your hands. We really hope this attractive addition to your bookshelf will inspire you to build many things on your own!

Armelle

mocassin serre-tête_

Contents

Projects for Cats

Projects for Cats

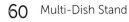

Projects for Cats and Dogs

Projects for Dogs

Practical Basics

Materials

In this book, the main construction material used is wood—not fine wood, but wood that is easy to find, such as pine. Out of respect for the environment, we never use exotic woods. We sometimes use wood products, such as oriented strand board (OSB), which is easy to work with and affordable. It's also aesthetically appealing and works really well with the uncluttered and understated current trends in home decorating. Plywood is another readily available option, and is often stronger than pine or OSB. You can also substitute particleboard, which is a little weaker, in some cases (but not for outdoor use).

All the other materials referenced in this book are easy to find at your local hardware store or home improvement store. As we are advocates for human contact when shopping, we believe a good merchant or salesperson will give you very good advice in selecting materials, so don't be shy—ask for help and recommendations, and bring this book along while you shop!

Tools

You will notice that the tools we use are fairly common. They are also essential if you intend to build things yourself. Here are the four basic types of tools you'll need.

Sandpaper. Sandpaper comes in different grits: fine grits for delicate and precise work, coarse grits for sanding or stripping. Having sheets of a few different grits on hand will make your work easier.

Saws. The first saw you will need is the jigsaw. Make sure you also buy **plastic safety goggles**. These will protect your eyes from flying debris and allow you to keep your eyes open, which in turn will help you keep your fingers out of harm's way and help you saw accurately. Along with the jigsaw, you will need a **handsaw** and a **miter box** for making straight and angled cuts.

Power drill. You can't build a lot of things without this tool. Almost all cordless power drills will accept both **drill bits** and **screwdriver** bits so that you can drill holes and drive screws with just one tool. You will need a variety of different sizes of bits, often included in the kit. If you're purchasing a drill, choose a cordless battery-powered drill. If you have a cordless screwdriver, it is helpful, but it's not a required purchase. Start by drilling a few holes in a scrap piece of wood to get used to handling the power tool. You shouldn't have much trouble mastering it after a few minutes of practice.

Screws. These essential items can vary a lot in style and size. Buy wood screws for the building projects in this book. For some pieces, you may want to use black screws, which are more aesthetic and will blend in with your décor. Look for small diameters (so that you won't see large screw heads everywhere). You will need a variety of screw lengths to make all the projects in this book. If you can, buy an assortment to always have a variety on hand. Otherwise, carefully review each project to ensure you select the best screws for the job before beginning. In general, screws should be long enough that you can get 1 to 1½ in (2.5 to 4 cm) of threads into the board you're screwing to (as long as the board is thick enough to accommodate that).

To prevent wood from splitting when using screws, it's important to drill pilot holes first—don't just drill the screws straight into the wood. Drill pilot holes for every project in this book to ensure the best results.

Colors

We intentionally limited the colors used in the projects in this book. Our objective was not to save money on paint or brushes, but to make it easier for you to picture these pieces in your own home. Keeping them depersonalized here allows you to imagine how you will decorate them to your own taste. We can, however, advise you on a few points regarding the paints you will use.

First of all, the second coat of paint is always the most important—don't neglect it. When the first coat of paint has dried, lightly sand the surface with fine-grit sandpaper. This will help the second coat of paint to adhere better.

If you want your project to be durable, don't skimp on the quality of your paint. A better brand of paint can often guarantee quality and durability. We tend to prefer matte colors that blend in well with minimalist or Scandinavian interiors, but use whatever works for you.

Many of these projects will look good painted. For a high-quality finish, we recommend that you do not skimp on your paintbrushes. Whatever the size, avoid the lowest-priced brushes. They will lose their bristles and leave indelible marks on your new piece of furniture. On large surfaces, use a roller to save time and distribute the paint evenly. To prevent streaks, don't forget to brush or roll the paint in one direction for the first layer, then in the opposite direction for the next layer.

PROJECTS
FOR
CATS

RADIATOR CAT BED

Difficulty
🐾

Did your cat disappear hours ago? Don't panic—he's probably curled up somewhere warm. Cats love cozy, out-of-the-way places. If you have radiators in your home, they may be the perfect place to hang a bed for your cat.

⚠ WARNING: This project is designed for hot-water radiators in homes heated by gas or oil (usually older houses and apartment buildings). Electric radiators can overheat and cause a fire if they come in contact with a combustible object.

MATERIALS

- 1 sheet OSB (oriented strand board)
- 2 furring strips, about 2 ft (60 cm) each
- 2 shelf brackets, minimum about 8 in (20 cm) on shortest arm
- 4 corner braces, about 2 to 3 in (5 to 7.5 cm)
- 2 nuts and bolts to fit the corner braces
- About 12 screws
- Fabric and foam
- Glue

TOOLS

- Power drill/screwdriver
- Staple gun and staples
- Saw
- Scissors

Making the bed

To prevent wood from splitting when using screws, it's important to drill pilot holes first—don't just drill the screws straight into the wood.

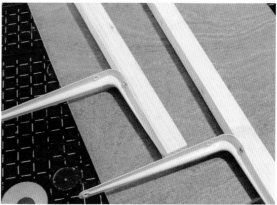

① Cut the furring strips to the desired length, referring to the photo of the finished project—you determine the distance between the top of the radiator and the bed.

② At the top of each furring strip, screw on a corner brace.

③ At the bottom of each furring strip, on the side opposite the one with the corner brace, screw on a shelf bracket.

Choose your corner braces carefully—their shape will determine the success of your project. Use metal corner braces, which will hold up better under pressure, heat, and repeated use.

④ At the top of each furring strip, use a nut and bolt to attach a second corner brace to the first corner brace to form a U; this is what will fit over the radiator.

⑤ Screw the board to the shelf brackets as shown. Make sure you choose a screw that is short enough not to go through the top of the board. If the screws do slightly break through, use adhesive putty to cover the tips.

If you can find someone to help you, this step is easier with two people.

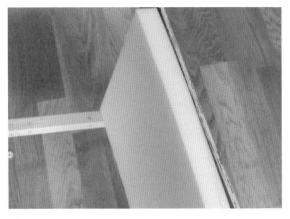

6 Glue the foam to the top of the board, cutting to foam to size as needed.

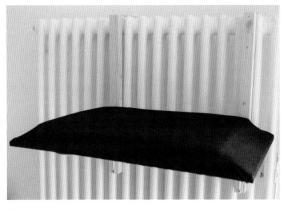

7 Lay the fabric over the foam, staple it to the underside of the board, and cut off any excess fabric.

In the end, this piece will have cost about $12, not counting the cost of heating—but who can put a price on keeping your cat warm and happy?

CAT TREE

Difficulty
🐾 🐾

Let's face it: most cat trees are ugly, with their outdated blue plush upholstery and cardboard construction that absorbs humidity and odors. As for the price, a basic model can easily set you back $100. Here's an example of a simple cat tree that is perfect for a small apartment and won't clash with your décor.

MATERIALS

- 1 wine crate
- 1 wooden tree stake, dowel, or PVC piping
- 1 board
- 1 screw
- About 100 ft (31 m) of cord
- Foam and fabric
- 3 long nails, about 6 in (15 cm)
- Concrete or mortar
- Paint (optional)

TOOLS

- Hole saw (same diameter as the stake), or jigsaw
- Power drill/screwdriver
- Staple gun and staples
- Glue gun and glue
- Scissors
- Trowel or large wooden stick (to mix concrete)
- Pencil

Making the base

1 Turn the wine crate upside down and trace two diagonal lines across the base from corner to corner to locate the exact center.

2 Using the hole saw, cut a hole in the center of the crate where the diagonal lines meet. Or use a jigsaw to cut a circle that is exactly the diameter of your stake.

Mark where the stake will sit in the hole in order to start wrapping it with cord in the next step—you don't want to wrap too much of the stake with cord and then have too little stake left to poke down into the crate.

3 Insert the stake in the hole you have cut.

4 If you want to paint the base of your cat tree, choose a color that blends in with your décor, and paint the base now.

Making the trunk

5 Wind the cord tightly and neatly around the stake and glue as you go, making sure to add glue at frequent, regular intervals.

Do not put cord all the way at the top of the post. Also, for best results, we recommend winding a second layer of cord over the first layer.

Making the top

6 Find the center of the board by tracing two diagonal lines across it. Screw the board to the top of the post, using the lines as a guide.

7 Glue the foam to the top of the board, cutting it to size as needed. Lay the fabric over the foam and staple it to the underside of the board. You can also staple a few long pieces of hanging cord to the underside to draw your cat's attention to this new plaything.

Finishing

To stabilize the base, you need to fill the wine crate with concrete. For this project, we mixed up mortar, which is stickier. Whatever product you decide to use, follow the manufacture's instructions for mixing.

8 Start by drilling a hole all the way through the stake, near the base where the stake emerges under the wine crate.

9 Drill a hole on each side of the crate.

10 Slide long nails (the longest you can find) into the holes. These nails will help the mortar (or concrete) stay in place inside the crate. Without the nails, the mortar will unmold when you turn the crate upside down.

11 Half fill the crate with mortar with the stake in place. Lightly tap the sides of the crate to help air bubbles escape. Let the piece dry vertically, in a dry area, for 48 hours.

Do not fill the crate completely, or it won't support the weight of the mortar. Half full is sufficient.

In the end, this piece will have cost you less than $20, with a little elbow grease and a lot of love for your cat!

WALL-MOUNTED SCRATCHING POSTS

Difficulty
🐾

Having an apartment cat sometimes means having to write off your furniture. Think of your shredded sofa or your upholstered chairs reduced to ribbons. To address this problem, we offer an alternative place for your cat to have fun that costs next to nothing to make. This project makes two posts.

MATERIALS

- 2 spools of cord
- PVC tubing, any diameter
- 2 wood brackets (sized to suit the PVC tubing)
- Screws (4 short and 4 long)
- Piece of cardboard (the flap from a cardboard box will work)

TOOLS

- Glue gun and glue
- Power drill/screwdriver
- Scissors
- Jigsaw (if you are cutting the PVC tubing yourself)
- Pencil

Cutting the pieces

1 Cut the PVC tubing to the desired length of the scratching post. Clearly mark the line where you will cut—with tubing, it's easy for the saw to slip and leave you whittling away at the end trying to even it out.

> Buy PVC tubes in the size you want, or just ask the home improvement store for scraps.

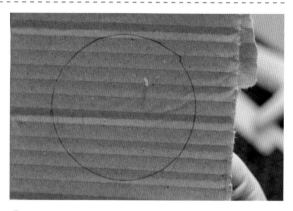

2 Cut a circle of cardboard in the same diameter as your tube (using the tube as a tracing template). This cardboard will be used to close the visible end of the tube.

> Don't glue the cardboard to the tube right away. Wait until the end of step 3.

Making the scratching posts

3 Wind the cord tightly and neatly around the PVC tube and glue as you go, making sure to add glue at frequent, regular intervals. Glue all the way to the end of the tube.

4 Glue the piece of cardboard to the end of the tube that will be visible. Then wind and glue the cord to the cardboard to fully cover the end of the tube.

> The easiest way to cover the cardboard end piece is to start by gluing one end of the cord to the center of the cardboard, then wind it outward toward the rim. You will be able to wind the cord more tightly this way.

Assembly

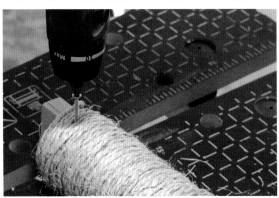

5 Fasten the bracket to the wall (we did not do this in the photos so that it would be easier for you to see the steps clearly). Place the wrapped tube on the bracket and screw both ends of the tube to the bracket.

Finishing

6 All that is left to do is wind a second layer of cord around the tube and then trim off any glue residue and imperfections. Your scratching post is done!

In the end, these posts will have cost less than $15 each.

BALCONY DINING TABLE

Difficulty
🐾

Some apartment dwellers let their cat spend time on the balcony to enjoy a taste of the outdoors. Our cat prefers to stay indoors, but for the more adventurous, here is a space-saving idea that combines the pleasure of an outdoor eating area with a convenient perch from which your cat can safely observe the world.

MATERIALS

- 2 decking boards (pressure-treated to prevent rot)
- 3 furring strips, 8 in (20 cm) long
- 2 small boards (length = combined width of 2 decking boards)
- 2 shelf brackets, no more than 6 in (15 cm) long on shortest arm
- 4 corner braces, about 2 to 3 in (5 to 7.5 cm)
- 2 nuts and bolts ($3/16$ in/5 mm diameter)
- About 21 screws

TOOLS

- Power drill/screwdriver

Preparing the brackets

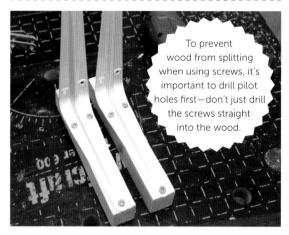

To prevent wood from splitting when using screws, it's important to drill pilot holes first—don't just drill the screws straight into the wood.

1 Screw the two shelf brackets onto two of the furring strips.

Make sure the furring strips are the same length.

Assembling the boards

2 Lay each short board across the back of the decking boards, one near each end, and screw them on, making sure the screws do not pierce the top side. This will secure your decking boards.

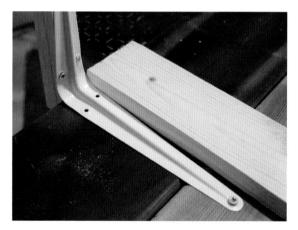

3 Keeping the secured decking boards upside down, position each attached shelf bracket and furring strip next to a supporting board. Screw on each shelf bracket.

Finishing

4 On the side of each furring strip opposite to the shelf bracket, screw on a corner brace. Then use a nut and bolt to attach a second corner brace to the first corner brace to form a U; this is what will fit over the railing.

5 Measure and mark the center point of your table, then screw on a third furring strip parallel to the other two. Add one or more wood spacers if necessary, according to the width of your balcony railing. To make wood spacers, cut pieces from extra furring strips.

The goal is to keep the table level.

In the end, this project will have cost less than $12. And if your cat's acrobatics make you too nervous, you can use this little dining table for yourself!

SCRATCHING PANELS

Difficulty

Having torn carpeting is no laughing matter. These attractive panels are a low-cost distraction for your cat, especially if you are a tenant who wants to keep your landlord's place in good condition.

MATERIALS

- Large piece of industrial carpeting (in a mottled color)
- 3 wood picture frames (with backing)
- 6 screws

TOOLS

- Power drill/screwdriver
- Scissors
- Utility knife
- Glue gun and glue
- Pencil

Making the panels

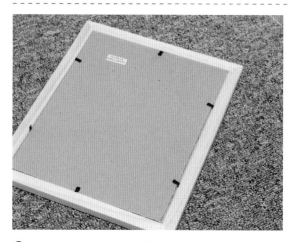

① Remove the glass, any filler paper, and the backing from the picture frames.

> Keep the backing. You can discard the filler paper and glass (safely).

② Use the backing as a template to trace three panels of carpeting. Cut the carpet panels out with a utility knife, then use scissors to trim the edges as needed.

③ Place each piece of carpet in a frame to test the fit. It should fit in perfectly. Once you've verified the fit, glue each carpet panel to a backing and secure the panel in the frame. Take extra care to glue around all the edges so that the panel doesn't pull up as your cat scratches it.

④ Drill a hole on two opposite corners of each frame. Place the frames on the wall in your desired arrangement, at a height your cat's claws can comfortably reach, then screw the frames to the wall to secure them.

In the end, these panels will have cost about $7 each.

SEAT WITH HIDDEN LITTER BOX

Difficulty
🐾 🐾

This piece of furniture is easy to build and can serve as a focal point in your room. An eye-catching combination of rectangular and round shapes, it's comfortable, compact, and, best of all, a clever way of hiding an unattractive litter box while still making it easy to maintain daily. OSB is a very trendy look in decorating, adding a homey-chic touch to your surroundings. It's also a material that is easy to work with.

MATERIALS

- 3 OSB (oriented strand board) panels, 48 x 24 in (120 x 60 cm)
- 2 OSB (oriented strand board) panels, 24 x 24 in (60 x 60 cm)
- 4 furring strips, 79 in (2 m) long, 2 x 2 in (5 x 5 cm) wide
- 12 corner braces, about 2 to 3 in (5 to 7.5 cm)
- About 30 screws
- 2 hinges for the lid

TOOLS

- Power drill/screwdriver
- Jigsaw (a router is ideal for cutting a perfect circle)
- Fine-grit sandpaper
- Tape measure
- Pencil
- String

Cutting the boards

1 The first step is to cut the OSB panels to size. We had this done at our local home improvement store. It's not expensive and is easier than trying to cut them at home. If you do want to save money, however, you can cut them yourself.

> WARNING: OSB leaves small splinters. Be sure to sand it with fine-grit sandpaper to make it smoother. Don't forget the edges, but don't sand with too much force or you'll shave down your measurements!

Cutting the opening

2 Choose a 48 x 24 in (120 x 60 cm) panel and use a pencil to trace a line dividing the panel in half, into two 24 x 24 in (60 x 60 cm) squares. On one half, trace diagonal lines to determine the center of the circle to be cut out.

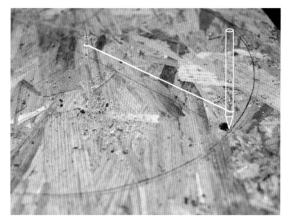

3 Drill a screw in the center of the square. Use string and pencil like a compass to trace a 10 in (25 cm) circle.

4 Using a large drill bit, drill a hole on the inside edge of the circle that is wide enough to insert the blade of the jigsaw. Saw along the line of the circle to completely cut it out. Sand to remove splinters around the rim.

Making the frames

5 Make three 24 x 24 in (60 x 60 cm) frames using the furring strips. (Follow the same steps as you would for the Protective Window/Door Net on page 46.) These frames will be set inside the bench. This will reinforce the bench so you can sit on it without wondering if you will land in your cat's litter box.

Assembling the panels

6 Position the front, back, and side OSB panels with the frames as shown in the photo (also see page 45). The lid will be attached separately.

7 Screw on the panels, making sure to take into account the width of the panel that is perpendicular to the one you are screwing on. In the end, the exterior of the piece should be flush and smooth.

Making the lid

8 Center each hinge between two frames, then, using short screws, fasten the hinges in the closed position on the inside of the bench. This will ensure you have a properly centered lid.

Finishing

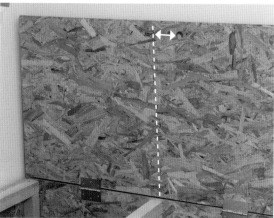

9 If you want to make it easier to lift the lid, use a flat drill bit to cut a hole in the lid as shown. Make sure to drill the hole slightly off-center—if the hole is in the center, you won't be able to insert your finger, because the center frame will be blocking the hole. Sand the bench.

In the end, this piece of furniture will have cost about $100 in materials.

PROTECTIVE WINDOW/ DOOR NET

Difficulty
🐾 🐾

Protecting your cat is a daily concern, especially when you live on an upper floor in a city and you also want fresh air. Building a protective net for your cat is simple, and the net will not cut down the amount of light coming into the room. You can air out your home while allowing your cat a little more freedom.

MATERIALS

- About 20 screws
- 4 corner braces, about 2 to 3 in (5 to 7.5 cm)
- Metal tabs
- Netting (enough for your window/door)
- 4 furring strips, 79 in (2 m) long, 1 x 1 in (2.5 x 2.5 cm) wide (this was what we needed for our large window)

TOOLS

- Carpenter's square
- Saw
- Staple gun and staples
- Power drill/screwdriver
- Phillips head screwdriver
- Scissors
- Tape measure
- Pencil

Measuring and cutting the furring strips

1 First, take measurements. Calculate the size of the inside of your window frame to accommodate the frame you will build, and figure out the length of each of the four strips you will need to cut.

Don't forget to subtract the width of the furring strip from two of the strips for an assembly as shown in the photo (see step 4).

2 Mark each furring strip to the lengths you need from step 1, then use the carpenter's square to trace a straight line across the furring strip where you will cut with the saw.

3 Once the furring strips have been cut, you can assemble them on the floor to check the fit before you attach anything.

Assembling the frame

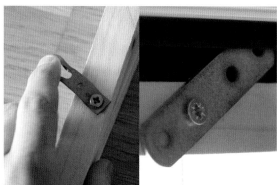

4 Screw the furring strips together using the corner braces as shown. Use short screws that will not stick out on the other side of the furring strips.

5 Using the manual screwdriver, screw on the metal tabs without forcing them down too much. They will serve as latches to squeeze into the inside frame of your window.

6 Test the frame in your window before installing the net. This will allow you to make any corrections to the frame if necessary.

Attaching the net

7 Staple the net to the frame as straight as possible, leaving a little extra netting along each edge to prevent tearing as you go (one extra square will likely be sufficient).

8 Use scissors to cut off the extra netting.

It can cost less than $35 to build a frame for a large window.

ROLLING LITTER BOX CABINET

Difficulty
🐾

Here is a practical way to disguise your cat's litter box while keeping it accessible. This attractive piece fits in nicely with most modern kitchens and is easy to build. You may even discover other places and uses for this unobtrusive rolling cabinet.

MATERIALS

- 1 kitchen cupboard/cabinet unit with door
- 4 wheels
- Screws (enough for the wheels)

TOOLS

- Power drill/screwdriver, including a large drill bit
- Jigsaw
- Carpenter's square
- Dinner plate
- Sandpaper
- Pencil

Tracing the opening

1 Start by tracing two vertical lines on one side of the cupboard, starting at the bottom. Space the lines at an equal distance from each edge and draw them to the desired height. Here, we opted for a height of 12 in (30 cm). Use a carpenter's square to ensure the lines are symmetrical.

Remember: Do not cut into an area that already has screws. Check before cutting.

2 Place the dinner plate at the top of the two lines and trace around its edge to form a curve at the top of the opening.

Cutting the opening

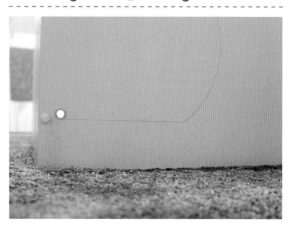

3 Use the drill with a sufficiently wide drill bit to cut a hole wide enough to insert your jigsaw on the inside of the opening you've drawn.

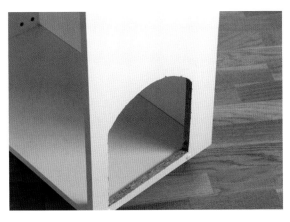

In the end, this piece of furniture will have cost about $35 and not much effort, and you'll have made daily life more pleasant.

④ Slide the blade of the jigsaw into the hole and saw along the line. Cut slowly to follow the curve accurately.

Don't forget to sand around the cut rim! This is an important step. The beauty of your cabinet and your pet's comfort are at stake!

Finishing

⑤ Turn the piece upside down and mark a reference point at each of the four corners that is an equal distance from the edges. Screw on the wheels.

WALL-MOUNTED CAT PLAYHOUSE

Difficulty
🐾

This playhouse for your cat is easy to build, is practical, and promises hours of enjoyment. You can decorate it to match your surroundings and even make it a focal point in your cat's favorite part of the house.

MATERIALS

- 2 boards, 26 in (65 cm) long and about 12 in (31 cm) wide
- 2 shelf brackets, minimum about 8 in (20 cm) on shortest arm
- About 17 screws

TOOLS

- Jigsaw
- Ruler and/or carpenter's square
- Pencil
- Sandpaper
- Power drill/screwdriver
- Small dinner plate

Making the opening

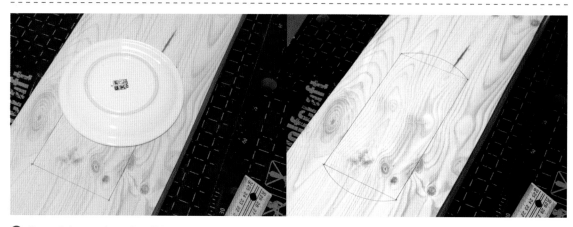

1 One of the two boards will have a window for your cat. Measure a rectangle in the size you wish on one of the boards and use a pencil to trace the outline. To get the curved shape on the sides, place the plate upside down on the board and trace it on each end of the rectangle.

2 Next, drill four holes with a drill bit that will be wide enough for you to insert the blade of the jigsaw. Make these holes on the inside of the four corners of the rectangle.

Drill the four holes before beginning to cut. That will save you from having to put down the jigsaw each time, and will also help you cut more accurately.

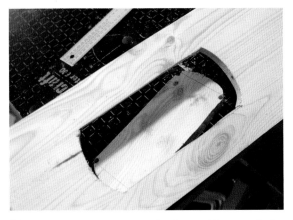

3 Cut the window out with the jigsaw. Then sand all the edges to make them smooth.

Assembling the boards

4 Pre-drill the second board where the two boards will meet to make a right angle. Screw them together using several screws all along the edge.

Finishing

5 Once the boards are attached to one another, attach the two shelf brackets to the piece, making sure that the part of the bracket facing the wall is perfectly flat.

You can also attach the brackets to the wall first, then attach the shelf to the brackets.

In the end, this piece of furniture will have cost about $10 and will entertain your cat for years to come!

MULTI-DISH STAND

Difficulty
🐾 🐾

This practical stand makes it easy to keep all your cat's dishes together and move them to another area all the same time. Its simple design will blend in easily with your décor. There is even a space for a cat-friendly potted plant!

MATERIALS

- 2 furring strips, 100 in (250 cm) long, 1 x 1 in (2.7 x 2.7 cm) wide
- About 30 screws

TOOLS

- Wood saw
- Power drill/screwdriver
- Fine-grit sandpaper (or choose furring strips that have already been sanded)
- Tape measure
- Pencil

Preparing the frame

1 Cut the furring strips to the dimensions you need in order to create a piece that follows the structure shown in the photos and that fits your cat's dishes.

Make a plan, detailing and calculating all the measurements and taking into account the widths of the furring strips and the rims of the dishes, as well as their depth. Taking careful measurements now will help save you time during construction. It will also help you avoid mistakes and waste materials, which will save you money! Use the photo of the assembled frame here to guide you in drawing up the plan.

Cut out all the pieces at the start. You can use the first piece as a template, to save time cutting and to avoid having to take out the tape measure every few seconds.

Assembling the furring strips

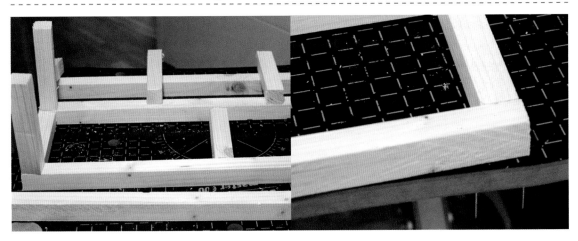

2 Assemble the furring strips to see what the size of your stand will be at the end. This will help you avoid mistakes before you start screwing the pieces together. Sand the furring strips at this stage.

3 Once you are satisfied with the placement, pre-drill holes for all the screws using a small drill bit.

Drill slowly. Later, when you are screwing, hold the furring strips firmly together to prevent them from shifting.

④ Start by assembling the two main rectangles (the base and top of your stand). Then continue with the vertical supports.

Finishing

Shift the vertical pieces about ½ in (1.5 cm) in toward the inside of the frame so that the screws do not collide with each other.

⑤ Set the dishes in place and let your cat get familiar with the new stand. You can also paint the stand; use an eco-friendly, nontoxic paint, and make sure the paint is thoroughly dry before using the stand.

In the end, this piece of furniture will have cost less than $12 in screws and furring strips.

PROJECTS
FOR
CATS AND DOGS

TRAVEL BASKET

Difficulty

Pet stores sell all kinds of carriers for cats and small dogs. They are often made of plastic and have mesh doors. They're not very pretty and aren't useful for any other purpose. Here is a way to transform your Sunday market wicker basket into an attractive and unique carrier for your pet.

MATERIALS

- Wicker basket
- About 65 ft (20 m) of cord
- 1 piece OSB (oriented strand board) or plywood (minimum ½ in/1 cm thick)

TOOLS

- Power drill/screwdriver (with a medium drill bit)
- Jigsaw
- Tape measure
- Pencil
- Scissors
- Sandpaper

Cutting out the lid

1 Trace the outline of your basket in pencil on the wood. There's no need to make a perfect circle—your basket is not a perfect circle, and, in any case, this wood won't show once it is wrapped in cord.

> If the top of the basket is not the same size as the bottom, trace the top of the basket onto a piece of cardboard, then use the cardboard as a template to trace a circle onto the wood.

2 Drill a hole inside your drawn circle, at least 2 in (5 cm) in from the circle's edge. Slide in the blade of your jigsaw and cut a circle inside the drawn circle. If you want to freehand the inner circle before you cut it, feel free. Then cut out around the original drawn circle as well so that you have a hoop.

3 Your circle doesn't have to be perfect. You just need a hoop that is wide enough to drill holes in every 1 in (2.5 cm) along.

> Check that the hoop will be usable for the lid of the basket at this point. If it is slightly wider—no more than ½ in (1 cm)—it's fine. Otherwise, you will need to adjust the hoop you've made, or start over again with a new piece of wood.

Making the lid

4 Sand the edges of the hoop—even though it will be covered in cord, you still need to prevent the wood from splintering. After sanding, drill holes every 1 in (2.5 cm) along the entire hoop.

5 Use the cord to weave the lid, crossing back and forth in whatever pattern you like. Make sure you weave the cord closely together to keep your pet from escaping. Stretch the cord tightly.

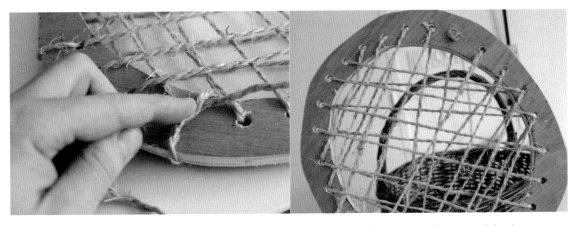

6 Once you have finished weaving, tie a double or triple knot in the ends of the cord to secure it in place.

7 Now the patient work begins. Use the cord to wrap and completely cover the wooden hoop. To make this easier, cut the cord into 6 ft (2 m) lengths. When you get to the end of a length, use the next piece of cord to cover the end of the previous length and hold it in place underneath the hoop. This technique will prevent unsightly knots and bulges.

8 Place the lid on top of the basket, in a closed position, to check the fit and alignment before continuing to step 9.

Assembly

9 Cut three pieces of cord that measure 10 in (25 cm) each. Use two of them to make two hinges as shown in the photo, through the wicker basket itself and around the hoop.

10 Use the third cord to create the lid closure by tying it to the opposite side of the hoop from the hinges and around the handle so it can slide up and down the handle.

In the end, this basket will have cost less than $10, not counting the basket itself and perhaps a cushion inside for comfort. It takes time and patience, but this unique piece will make you stand out in a crowd of plastic pet carriers!

TEEPEE BED

Difficulty
🐾 🐾 🐾

We are fond of the teepee motif and delighted by the return of light wood in home decoration. Here, they come together in an airy and understated bed for your cat or dog. Quick and easy to build, this wood teepee is a simple alternative to a fabric teepee for those who don't use a sewing machine.

MATERIALS

- 1 pine board, 78 in (2 m) long x 15 in (40 cm) wide
- 4 screws
- 1 piece of carpeting

TOOLS

- Power drill/screwdriver
- Jigsaw
- Tape measure
- Carpenter's square
- Sandpaper
- Pencil

Cutting the wood

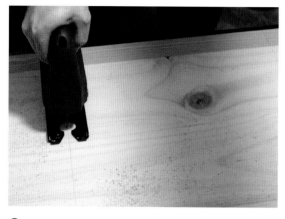

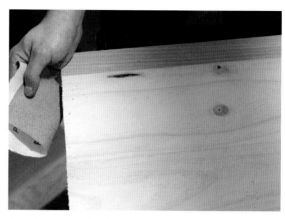

1 To cut a pine board, all you need is to take all your measurements end to end and then use a jigsaw to make the cuts. Cut three pieces total: two boards of 30 x 15 in (80 x 40 cm) for the walls of the teepee and one of 15 x 15 in (40 x 40 cm) for the base.

Remember to sand the edges to remove splinters and make them smooth to the touch.

You can have the boards cut at the home improvement store for a nominal fee. This will keep you from making a mess at home if you aren't fortunate enough to have a workshop.

Cutting out the slot

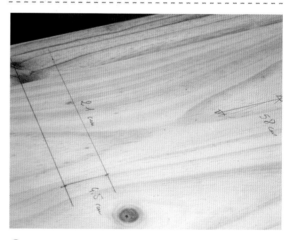

2 Next, trace the slot cutout measurements directly on the boards. At 23 in (58 cm) in from one end of each of the two larger wall sections, trace a slot coming from the edge that is 8¼ in (21 cm) long and 1¾ in (4.5 cm) wide. See the photo for a model to follow.

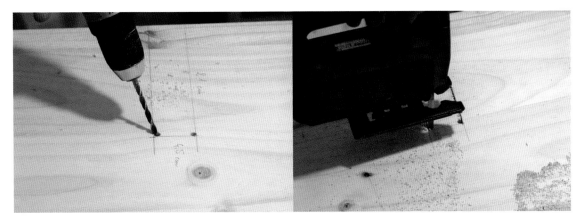

3 Next, drill two holes right on the two inside corners of each of the slots to help make it easier to pivot the jigsaw.

4 Cut out both slots completely.

Remember to sand again for a clean, splinter-free finish.

Making the base

5 Fit the two walls together securely as shown in the photos, then measure the size of the base at the same height on each wall board where you want to attach the base board.

6 Pre-drill four holes, two on each side, then screw on the base board as shown here and below left.

7 You can decorate the teepee as you like. If this is for a cat, add a piece of carpeting to one of the outside walls to use as a scratching post.

In the end, this piece will have cost less than $12.

ROLLING END TABLE BED

Difficulty
🐾 🐾

Recycling and resourcefulness capture the spirit of DIY in this little project—a rolling end table that doubles as a cozy pet bed, built from scrap pieces of OSB. It's proof that an inexpensive, homemade piece of furniture can fit in perfectly with current decorating trends.

MATERIALS

- OSB (oriented strand board) scraps from a home improvement store (see page 82)
- About 28 screws
- 4 wheels

TOOLS

- Power drill/screwdriver
- Jigsaw
- Sandpaper
- String
- Pencil
- Tape measure

Selecting the OSB pieces

1 The first step takes place at your local home improvement store. Plan to spend a little time here. Most home improvement stores have a scrap wood section, usually near the department where they cut wood for you. None of these scraps are in standard sizes, but, with a little patience and creativity, you can walk out with some inexpensive materials. For this project, we used OSB, which is very much in style right now. It fits in nicely with understated, Scandinavian, and ethnic-chic décor.

Take the time to put the pieces together, without screws, by just using the scraps you find in the store. You may look a little odd, but it will help ensure you have sufficient material before you head home.

Plan to spend some time sanding your scrap OSB. It's not the most difficult or unpleasant task, but it's important to take this into account.

2 Once you have the OSB pieces, take the time to do a rough assembly, putting the pieces together without screws.

We found the wood we needed in order to get these measurements:

- 2 pieces, 15 x 19 in (38.5 x 48 cm), for the top and base
- 2 pieces, 19 x 16 in (48 x 41 cm), for the sides
- 2 pieces, 15 x 15 in (38.5 x 38.5 cm), for the front and back

These measurements are just examples. You will need to work with what you find in the scrap wood section—and also the size of your pet.

Assembling the piece

3 This next step is easier if you have a helper, unless you are willing to go into contortions worthy of Russian gymnasts. Hold the pieces together and screw them into place, leaving out the panel you want to use as the top surface of the end table.

4 At this stage, you have a large, open box. Choose the side where the opening will be (remember, the open face of the box will become the top surface). Trace diagonal lines across it to find the center. (To keep it simple, we chose the square side.)

Making the opening

5 Insert a screw where you have marked the center of the panel. Tie a string to the screw and tie a pencil to the other end of the string. Use this DIY compass to trace the circular opening. We recommend that you tie the string as close to the bottom of the pencil as possible to avoid deviating from a perfect circle.

6 Once the circle is traced, use the drill to make a hole inside the circle, along the traced line. The hole should be wide enough to insert the blade of your jigsaw.

7 Once you have drilled the hole, slide the blade of your jigsaw in and carefully saw along the line to completely cut out the circle.

Don't forget to sand after each cut.

8 Turn the box upside down. Position the wheels at the 4 corners without screwing them in to see if everything looks right. When you are satisfied, screw them in.

9 Turn the box right side up and screw on the top piece. Sand all the edges of this piece until you have a nice, soft finish that won't injure your pet.

The main advantage of this piece in the end is its cost—less than $20!

SCANDINAVIAN-STYLE BED

Difficulty
🐾

How sweet it is to live in a space where all the furniture goes together and captures the same spirit. When it comes to ready-made pet furniture, finding something pretty yet unobtrusive can be difficult. Here's a bed for your dog or cat that will fit in perfectly with Scandinavian décor.

MATERIALS

- 4 beveled bed legs
- 4 nuts and bolts ($\frac{5}{16}$ in/8 mm in diameter)
- 1 board, 24 x 15 in (60 cm x 40 cm)
- 2 boards, 15 x 6 in (40 x 15 cm)
- 1 board, 24 x 6 in (60 x 15 cm)
- About 10 screws

TOOLS

- Power drill/screwdriver
- Jigsaw
- $\frac{5}{16}$ in (8 mm) ratcheting wrench

Cutting the boards

1 Cut the boards to the desired lengths and according to the size of your pet. In our measurements, we planned to leave a little edge protruding at the front, but you can eliminate this edge if you want by adding the thickness of the board to your measurements. (See the final photo for how the pieces fit together.)

> You can have the boards cut at a home improvement store to avoid making a mess at home and to be sure you'll have perfect cuts. But remember, this service is not free.

Assembling the bed

2 Next, assemble the boards without screwing them together. This will help you see what the volume of the piece will be and allow you to check that the measurements are correct.

3 Once you are happy with the fit of the bed, screw the boards together, starting by screwing the two sides to the base of the bed, then screwing the back piece on.

Finishing

4 Turn the piece upside down and mark reference points for the legs that are at equal distances from the four corners. We chose to position the legs 1½ in (4 cm) from the edges. Drill holes at these points and position the legs.

5 Screw the bolt to each leg, and the bed is done!

In the end, this piece of furniture will have cost less than $25.

PROJECTS
FOR
DOGS

DISH STAND WITH BUILT-IN STORAGE

Difficulty
❧ ❧

If you have a fairly large dog, the choice of dog dishes can be limited. Unfortunately, not too many companies spend time designing products for dogs that are both practical and aesthetically pleasing, especially for dogs that don't look like miniature stuffed toys. To make up for this, we'll help you make this piece of furniture with a drawer for dog food that will also hold your large dog's dish.

MATERIALS

- 1 wine crate
- 4 furring strips, 7 in (18 cm) long
- 4 furring strips, 12½ in (31.6 cm) long
- 5 furring strips, the length of your wine crate
- About 20 screws
- 1 board

TOOLS

- Power drill/screwdriver (with wide drill bit and flat drill bit)
- Saw
- Jigsaw
- Miter box
- Sandpaper
- Pencil
- Cloth tape measure

Preparing the frame

1 Cut the furring strips to the dimensions indicated (use a miter box for perfectly straight cuts). Assemble the 7 in (18 cm) and 12½ in (31.6 cm) furring strips to form two frames as shown. These dimensions work for our wine crate, but check to make sure that your dimensions will work for yours (see step 2).

2 Check that the wine crate slides easily through both frames. It is important to check at this stage, because adjusting the frame will involve much less work now than later on.

> These furring strips are not the precise lengths and widths of the wine crate. It is better to measure a little longer on all sides so that the wine crate drawer can slide easily inside the frame.

> Remember to pre-drill the furring strips before screwing them together. Furring strips are fragile and risk splitting if you insert screws without drilling the holes first.

Assembling the frame

3 Next, connect the two frames using two of the wine crate–length furring strips, one on each side along the tops of the frames. These should screw on just underneath the 12½ in (31.6 cm) strips. (In this photo, the frame is horizontal on top, with the crosspiece being screwed on perpendicularly.) Remember to pre-drill.

4 Attach a third wine crate—length furring strip at the base of the frame, in the center. The wine crate will slide across this center piece.

It's better if you have two people at this stage, to keep the frame from shifting and the drawer from getting stuck in the frame.

5 Slide the crate into the frame to make sure it fits well. Then screw on the last two wine crate—length furring strips to the top of the frame to fill the space above the strips you screwed on in step 3. (See steps 6 and 7 for a visual of the final furring strip placement.)

Making the top

6 Position the board on top of the completed frame. Trace the corners of the frame onto the board to determine the final size you'll need for the top.

7 Cut the board, following the traced lines, then lay the board on top of the frame. Sand the top of the frame to ensure the board rests flat, then sand the edges of the board until smooth.

8 Trace diagonal lines across the board to find the center. Using a cloth tape measure or just a piece of string, measure the circumference of your dog bowl just underneath its rim, then trace a circle of that circumference onto the center of the board. (In the photo, we traced the base of our bowl, then cut a slightly larger circle, since our bowl was nearly straight-sided.)

9 Using a large drill bit, drill a hole just inside the drawn circle, insert the blade of your jigsaw, and cut out the circle. Don't forget to sand after cutting.

10 Pre-drill holes and screw the board to frame.

11 Check that the wine crate drawer pulls out completely and is not blocked by the base of the dish once the dish is placed in the hole. If the dish is in the way, cut a semicircle out of the back of the wine crate drawer to leave space for the dish. Use a large dinner plate as your template.

Finishing

12 Use a flat drill bit to drill a hole on the wine crate drawer end as shown. This will allow you to use your finger to easily pull out the drawer.

13 You can finish by oiling the piece.

In the end, this piece will have cost less than $25, combining practicality with the aesthetics of a handcrafted piece of furniture.

WALL-MOUNTED LEASH RACK

Difficulty
❖

Taking your dog for a walk is a part of everyday life, especially when you live in the city. Sometimes it's a pleasure, and sometimes it feels like a chore. To make it easier, this attractive rack holds all you need to get you and your dog out the door quickly and without forgetting the bags!

MATERIALS

- 1 board, 14 x 12 in (35 x 30 cm) (a scrap piece of wood is sufficient)
- 1 coat hook
- PVC tubing, about 8 in (20 cm) long
- 4 screws
- 4 screws/anchors/other fixatives to mount the rack to wall
- 1 roll of paper dog waste bags
- Spray paint

TOOLS

- Power drill/screwdriver
- Sanding block

Making the rack

1 Cut and sand the PVC tubing (or have it done at the home improvement store). Spray paint it black.

> Spray painting takes time and patience. Spray a very thin first layer, then let it dry for one hour before spraying a second layer. Continue like this until the color is satisfactory. Always wait one hour before spraying the next layer of paint, and always spray in a well-ventilated area.

2 Screw the coat hook onto the board in the desired position. Make sure not to use screws that are too long and that could stick out the other side of the board.

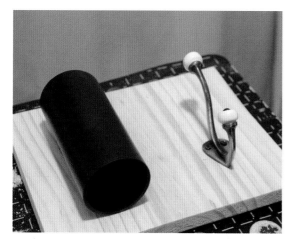

3 Position the PVC tube in the desired position, without screwing it in, to see what the rack will look like when it is finished.

4 Pre-drill holes to prevent the wood from splitting or the PVC tube from cracking. Screw the tube onto the board at an angle.

Finishing

5 Drill holes in the four corners of the board where it will be screwed onto the wall.

Always select the right screws and anchors for your type of wall (wood, brick, plasterboard, etc.).

6 Slide the roll of paper bags into the PVC tube. Unroll them slightly and pull out the end of one bag from the center of the roll. This will allow you to pull out one bag at a time. Depending on your bags, you may want to close up the base of the PVC tube with a circle of cardboard and hot glue to prevent the bags from falling out as you use them up.

7 Paint the piece according to your taste and interior décor. Use masking tape to outline the shapes and protect the parts that are not actively being painted.

In the end, this piece will have cost less than $20.

INDOOR DOGHOUSE

Difficulty
🐾 🐾

Cabin-frame beds are a popular trend in Scandinavian-style décor. Keeping in the same spirit, we've designed one your pet can enjoy as an indoor doghouse. You can paint it red like we have done, or a different color, or leave it the natural shade of the wood.

MATERIALS

- 4 furring strips, about 8 ft (2.4 m) long, minimum 3 in (76 mm) wide x 1½ in (38 mm) deep; alternatively, use 2 x 3 in (5 x 7.5 cm) studs
- About 30 screws

TOOLS

- Miter box
- Handsaw and/or pull saw
- Jigsaw
- Sandpaper
- Power drill/screwdriver
- Carpenter's square
- Pencil

Cutting the furring strips

① The first step is the messiest—sawing some of the furring strips (remember, there will be another sawing step later, too).
Cut the furring strips as follows:
• 4 long furring strips, 28 in (70 cm) long
• 2 medium furring strips, about 22 in (56 cm) long
• 4 short furring strips, 15½ in (40 cm) long

Make sure to sand each piece.

Cutting the angles

② Now you will need to cut angles in the four long furring strips. Place the furring strip in the miter box and line up the top of the furring strip with the top of the 45-degree angle on the miter box. Saw the wood, following the slots in the sides of the miter box. Repeat for each of the long furring strips.

③ Saw off the ends of the four short furring strips in the same way to ensure they will fit together against the long furring strips perfectly.

Assembling the angles

Group the cut furring strips into separate piles by length. Make sure you have cut the angles on the correct pieces!

4 Screw one short strip to one long strip at the cut angles, being sure to take into account the angles that will allow two furring strips to fit together tightly. See the right side of the step 5 photo for what you are assembling. Assemble all four pairs.

For a smooth and even finish, remember not only to sand each individual piece, but the entire structure once it is assembled.

To keep the wood from splitting, there are two solutions:
• use the power drill to pre-drill holes;
• use screws specially designed for this problem.

5 It's time to make the roof of the structure. You should obtain a 90-degree angle. One furring strip has to fit on top of the other one for each side, so you need to cut off the end of one piece that is equivalent to the width of the other. The result can be seen in this photo—the left-side top strip was shortened. Screw the two furring strips together at the peak. The front of the structure is taking shape.

6 Next, add one of the approximately 22 in (56 cm) medium furring strips to the bottom of one frame; you may need to trim this piece to size to make it the same width as the assembled top of the frame. The piece, in the end, should be perfectly parallel with all angles perfectly matched.

7 Assemble the back of the structure the same way. Then make sure that both front and back pieces match (line up) perfectly.

8 Next, decide the depth of the doghouse (which will depend on the size of your dog). Here we opted for 24 in (60 cm) in depth. Cut out five furring strips that are your chosen depth in length. You can relax now, because there are no more angles left to cut! Screw on a furring strip diagonally (as shown in the finished photo) at the very top peak, between the front and back frames. Then screw on two more furring strips diagonally (as shown in the finished photo) farther down, near the angled cuts, to reinforce the structure. Finally, add two furring strips at the base, sitting on top of the base strips added in steps 6 and 7, to form a rectangular shape (as shown in this photo). This will allow you to place a cushion in or on the base, or perhaps even a box.

In the end, this piece of furniture will have cost less than $15.

BICYCLE BASKET

Difficulty
🐾 🐾

Some people like to bring their dog everywhere with them—on walks, in the car, and even on a bicycle! For those of you on two wheels, here's a simple but unique way to transport pets and protect them from falls and other road mishaps.

MATERIALS

- 1 wood box (or wine crate)
- 4 furring strips, 28 in (70 cm) long
- 2 furring strips, 13 in (33 cm) long
- 2 furring strips, 8 in (20 cm) long
- About 20 screws
- 1 roll wire mesh
- 2 bungee cords
- 1 cord (or shoelace)

TOOLS

- Saw
- Miter box
- Staple gun and staples
- Wire cutters
- Power drill/screwdriver (with fine, medium, and flat ⅞ in/22 mm drill bits)
- Tape measure
- Pencil

Preparing the furring strips

1. Start by cutting the 8 furring strips to the measurements you'll need according to the dimensions of your box (the dimensions given in the materials list are the dimensions we used for our box, but you will need to determine your own):
   - 4 furring strips in the height of your box plus about 14 in (35 cm)
   - 2 furring strips in the length of your box (measuring inside the box)
   - 2 furring strips in the width of your box minus the total width of the two furring strips used for the length

   Trim the furring strips as needed, positioning them in the box to ensure they fit together perfectly (see the photo for step 4 as a positioning guide).

Making the structure

2. Position the four long furring strips in the corners of your box, pre-drill them, then screw them into the box.

Be careful not to tighten the screws too much.

3. Next, assemble the top of the frame. Position the two length-size furring strips lengthwise and the two width-size furring strips widthwise. Be careful not to screw the horizontal screws into the vertical screws.

4. Check all sides of the piece and sand every surface and edge. Make sure the frame is sturdy and ready for attaching the wire mesh screen.

Attaching the wire mesh screen

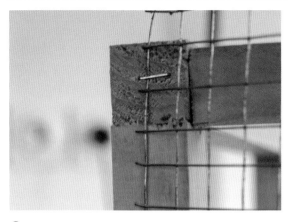

5 Staple one corner of the wire mesh to the frame as shown. Be sure to stretch the wire mesh before you staple it to the wood.

Remember to staple onto the vertical furring strips first, then the horizontal strips.

6 Close off the entire structure with mesh by stapling it to all the furring strips. Cutting in a straight line, trim off the excess mesh that sticks up at the top.

7 Remember to close the top of the basket as well.

8 Make an opening on one side by carefully cutting the screen on one of the wide sides of the basket, only cutting it on the bottom and sides so that you can lift it up and close it again.

Finishing

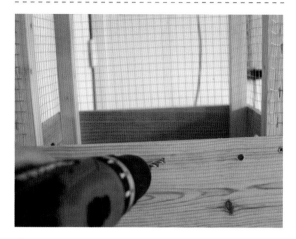

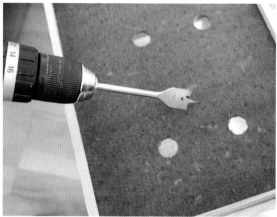

9 Make the fastening system by drilling three holes with a medium drill bit in the box along the side you cut away for the opening.

10 Use a flat drill bit to drill four holes in the bottom of the box for the bungee cords to pass through (see the photo below left).

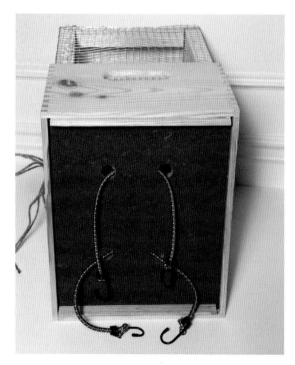

11 Use a piece of cord or a shoelace to close the opening of the basket when your pet is ready to travel.

In the end, it will have cost about $35 to protect your pet during your bicycle excursions.

CLASSIC DOGHOUSE

Difficulty
🐾 🐾 🐾

In furniture design for pets, there's still an appreciation for the timeless—especially if it keeps your dog out of the wind and rain. Here is a classic doghouse you can build with a minimal number of angled cuts.

MATERIALS

- Pine shelf board, total of 13 ft (4 m) long x 18 in (45 cm) wide x 1 in (2.5 cm) thick
- 2 furring strips, 6½ ft (2 m) long x 2½ in (64 mm) wide x 1¼ in (32 mm) deep; alternatively, use 2 x 3 in (5 x 7.5 cm) studs
- About 20 screws
- 1 can wood stain (optional)

TOOLS

- Power drill/screwdriver
- Jigsaw
- Miter box and handsaw
- Sandpaper
- Pencil
- Paintbrush (if using stain)

Cutting the furring strips

1 Cut the following lengths of furring strips:
- 4 strips of 18 in (45 cm)
- 4 strips of 12 in (30 cm)
- 2 strips of 13 in (33 cm)

Cut all the furring strips at the beginning. Then you will only have the assembling left to do.

Check carefully that all the furring strips are the same width and depth. If they are not, cut them to fit accordingly.

2 Next, trace and cut the angles. To do this, you need the miter box, a saw, and your full attention. Cut the ends of the four 12 in (30 cm) furring strips and the four 18 in (45 cm) furring strips at a 45-degree angle. It doesn't matter which angle, because you can turn the furring strip over before assembling it.

Making the frame

Check carefully that you are starting each cut at the very corner by looking at the cut from directly above.

3 Group the cut furring strips into separate piles by length. Good organization is key to a successful DIY project!

④ Assemble the pieces into two separate frame shapes using the Indoor Doghouse on page 102 as a model (referring to steps 4–7). Lay out the front and back angled long pieces, then the top angled short pieces, and finally two 13 in (33 cm) horizontal pieces for the base (see below). Screw the pieces together in that order, being sure to pre-drill.

As for the Indoor Doghouse (page 102), one of the furring strips must be cut shorter to create the perfect peak. This step comes after the initial cuts in order to help the wood fit together neatly. To do this, simply trace a line after placing one 12 in (30 cm) furring strip over another as shown, then saw.

Making the sides and the bottom

⑤ Once the frame is built, determine the measurements of the panels you will need (the two sides and the back), taking into account the thickness of the furring strips. Then cut the panels using the jigsaw. Use a guide for a straighter cut, if you can. Assemble the boards on the framework, starting with the two sides. Don't forget to always pre-drill holes before screwing the pieces together.

Have the boards cut for you at a home improvement store if you are concerned about making perfect cuts, or to avoid a big mess to clean up if you are working in an apartment.

Finishing

6 The hardest part is getting the roof to fit together perfectly. You may not get it right the first time, but simply recut the boards as needed to get that perfect fit.

7 Don't forget to fill in the back of the doghouse. We used the jigsaw to cut out a small triangle from scrap wood—it just took a few more measurements and a little geometry!

8 All that's left to do is to stain the doghouse, depending on the wood you used and where the doghouse will be located. A stain helps to preserve the wood in a damp climate.

In the end, this piece of furniture will have cost about $45 without the stain. Add on about $25 for a can of good quality wood stain.

TIRE BED

Difficulty

Dog baskets are all pretty much the same, with tufted cushions and fabric printed with the usual paws and bones motifs. Here is something a little more original. Making a bed from a tire might not seem very appealing, but we're sure that you'll love the style and that your dog will love the comfort.

MATERIALS

- 1 tire, used or new
- 1 cushion
- 1 board
- 4 screws
- Adhesive felt pads

TOOLS

- Power drill/screwdriver
- Jigsaw
- Pencil

Making the base

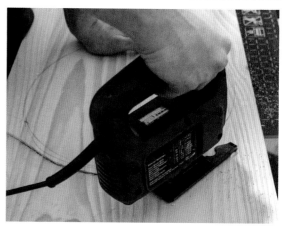

1 If you are using a used tire, clean it carefully, degreasing it and brushing it with a hard-bristled brush.

2 Trace the inside of the tire on the board, then draw another circle about 1½ in (3 cm) larger than the tire, making an outline around that first tire tracing.

3 Use the jigsaw to cut the circle out of the wood. This time, you want to preserve the circle itself, not the hole (as has been done in other projects).

Assembly

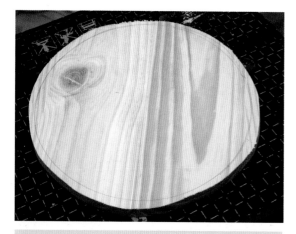

A perfect circle is not necessary—you just need the margin to be able to screw the circle to the tire.

4 Place the board under the tire for the base. Screw the tire to the board.

Finishing

5 Turn the piece upside down and attach several felt pads to the wood as shown. This will allow you to slide the bed easily across the floor and prevent the wood from scratching the floor.

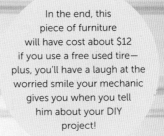

In the end, this piece of furniture will have cost about $12 if you use a free used tire—plus, you'll have a laugh at the worried smile your mechanic gives you when you tell him about your DIY project!

6 Place the cushion inside the tire bed.

About the Authors

Armelle Rau is a thirty-something style and décor enthusiast. She invigorates her world through her work as communications manager for a Scandinavian design network and also through her blog, *www.mocassinserretete.com*, which she has been passionately leading for four years.

Armelle can share her tastes and passions for hours with her readers on social networks—she is anything but stingy with advice to help her community to decorate their home spaces. Being an animal lover, Armelle tried her hand at building many projects for pets before writing this book.

Pierre Legrix, Armelle's partner, also in his thirties, is a French teacher who is passionate about DIY and home improvement and who supports Armelle and her various desires to create (and recreate!) their home.

Info, the couple's white and ginger cat, is four years old and seems amused to have been the object of so much attention during the creation of this book.

The trio were all born in Nantes, France, and live there in a 230 square ft (70 square m) 1960s apartment that has been renovated to suit their tastes. Inspired by Scandinavian design and bohemian chic style, they have filled their home with objects gathered during their travels and gleaned from flea markets.

Acknowledgments

Thanks to all our readers.

Thanks to our talented photographer, Pierre Nicou, who made our little creations look so wonderful. Thanks to our supporters and loved ones who encouraged us to do our very best, as they always have. Thanks to Catherine for her ideas and joyful enthusiasm for decorating that set us on the right track when we weren't sure how we'd get there.

Thanks to our cat, Info.

Thanks to my blog readers, who have supported me since the start of the "mocassin serre-tête" adventure and who commented on my photos and articles. I am truly grateful, because without you none of this would have been possible.

See you soon for more adventures on *www.mocassinserretete.com*.

Info

Note: Page numbers in *italics* indicate projects.